4TH GRADE US HISTORY THE CIVIL WAR YEARS

BABY PROFESSOR

EDUCATION KIDS

The Civil War was fought
between the Northern and the
Southern states from 1861-1865.

The American Civil War was fought between southern and northern states of the United States.

The Civil War was
the deadliest
war in American
history. There
were around
210,000 soldiers
killed in action
and 625,000
total dead.

CAMP MARIETTA
Co.
1507
CCC

There are many causes that led to the American Civil War. While slavery is generally cited as the main cause for the war.

Abraham Lincoln
was the President
of the United
States during
the Civil War.
He preserved
the Union,
abolished slavery,
strengthened
the federal
government,
and modernized
the economy.

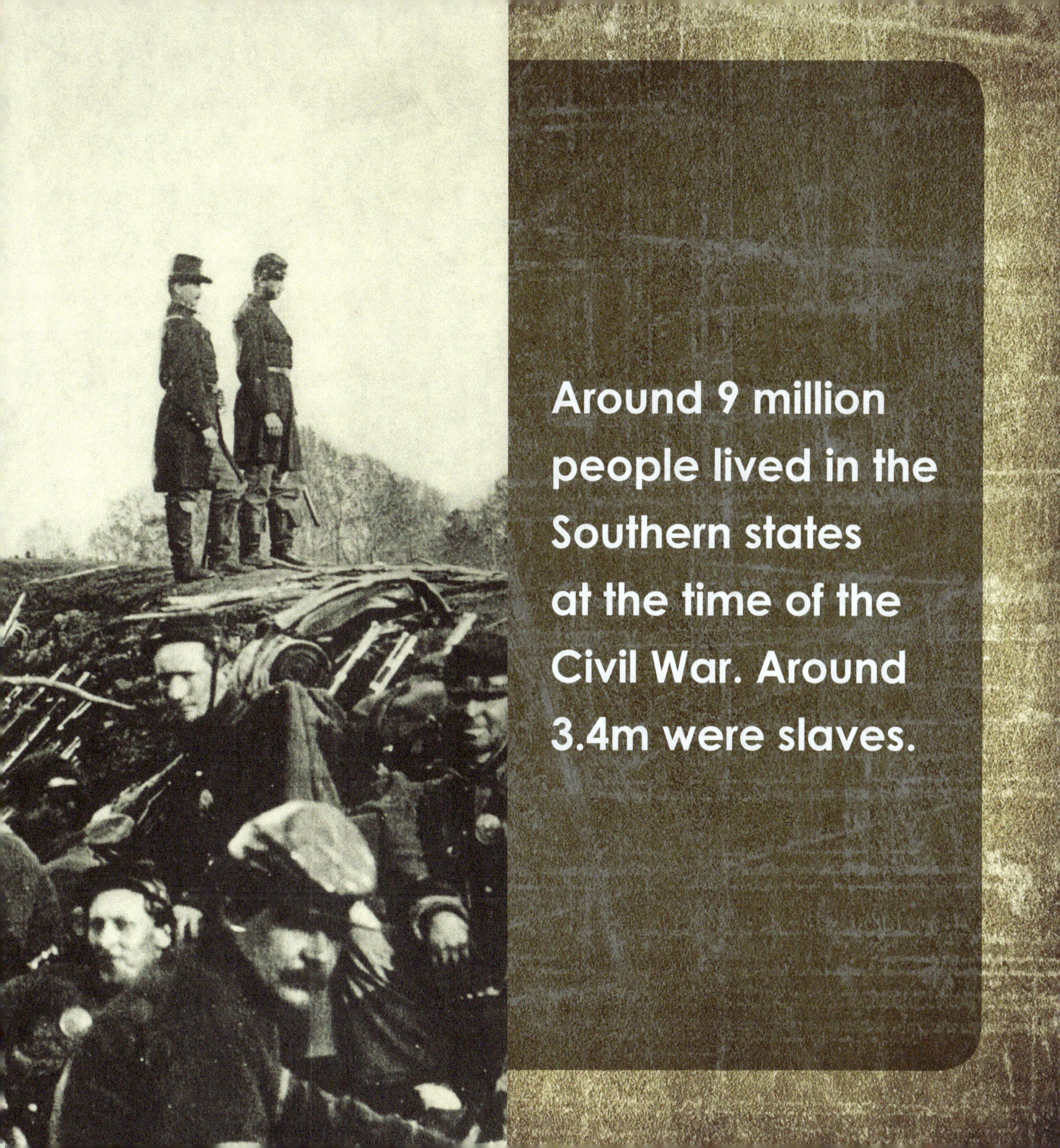
Around 9 million
people lived in the
Southern states
at the time of the
Civil War. Around
3.4m were slaves.

Lincoln dreamed of getting assassinated only a few days before he was killed by John Wilkes Booth.

After the war was over, the Constitution was amended to free the slaves, to assure "equal protection under the law" for American citizens, and to grant black men the right to vote.

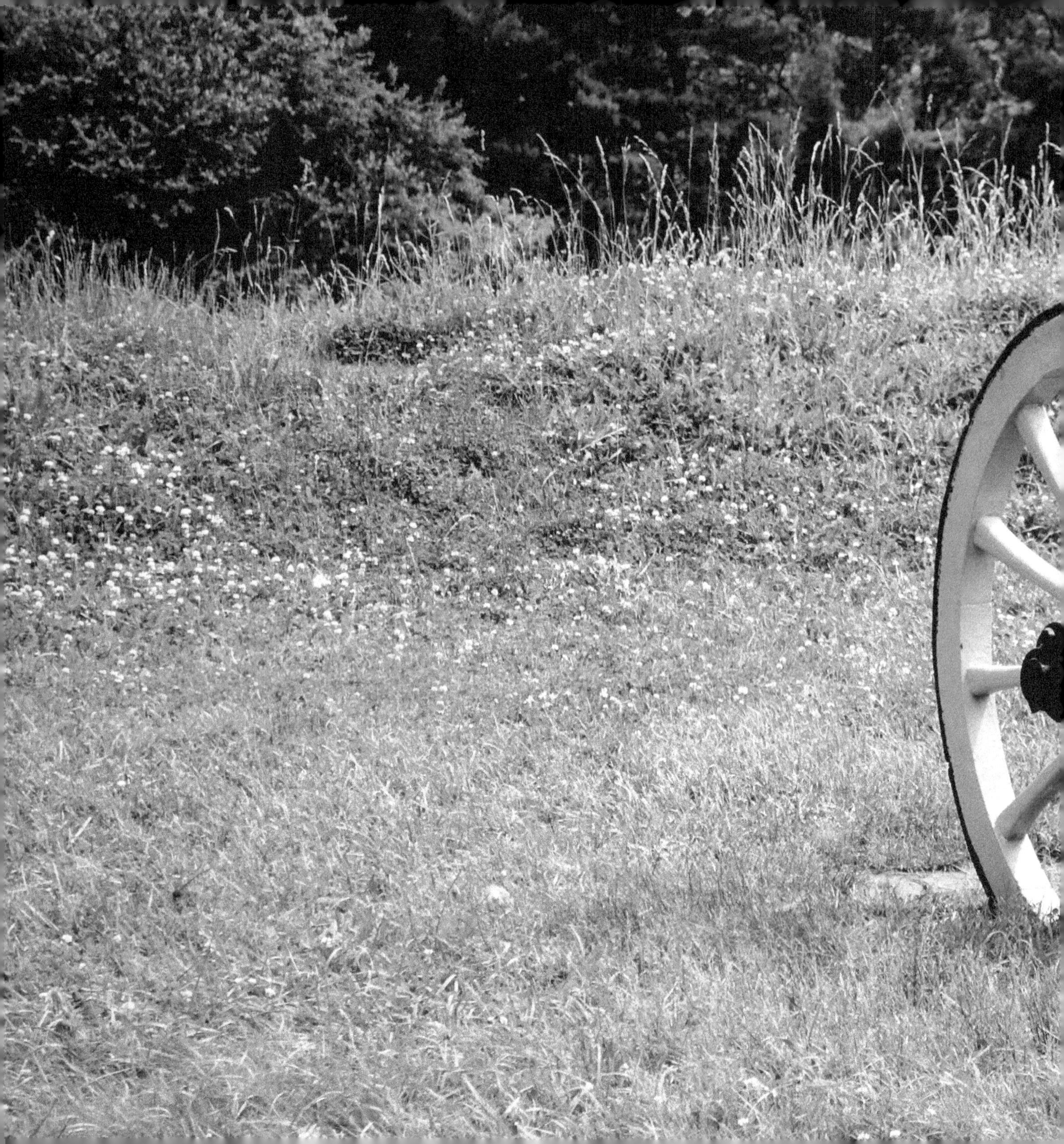